The Boy Who Became King

WRITTEN AND ILLUSTRATED
BY ANTHONY CURCIO

LeBron James

The Children's Book

Less than a week after Christmas in 1984, a young woman named Gloria received the best gift she could ever imagine, a baby boy she named LeBron. LeBron was born in the city of Akron, Ohio.

Gloria, her mother and even her grandmother all helped raise baby
LeBron. They all lived together in a big house until both women passed
away, leaving young Gloria and LeBron all on their own with no place
to stay.

It was hard for Gloria, moving from place to place, trying to work *and* take care of a young child without any help from LeBron's father, who left before he was born.

Gloria did her best, but it only became more difficult as LeBron got older. They always had to move from place to place because they didn't have enough money. One time, they moved *five times* in three months.

Often times Gloria would leave for work and an 8 year old LeBron was left at home by himself.

LeBron missed *a lot* of school. He would wake up, watch tv, play video games and even walk to the store on his own. He didn't want to go to school. He wasn't like the other 8 and 9 years olds who didn't have to worry about where they were going to sleep each night.

And when he did go to school, it wasn't easy for LeBron because he was always so far behind. Sometimes he would get sad because other kids had so much and he had so little.

They had nice clothes, *two* parents at home and they did well in school. All LeBron had was his mom and they were very, very poor.

All of the kids took off running as fast as they could. LeBron got a late start but one by one he passed them all, winning the foot race by what seemed like a mile.

The friendly coach, found Gloria and asked her if LeBron could play on his team.

"Playing on a football team would make my *Bron Bron* so happy and I would love that but there is no way I can afford it and I wouldn't be able to get him to all the practices," Gloria stated.

"Don't worry about any of that, I will take care of everything and I'll pick him up every day," replied the coach.

The very first time LeBron
touched the ball, he ran 80 yards
for a touchdown. He was a star!

Gloria would get off work on the weekends to come and watch LeBron's
games. She was his biggest fan and even became the team mom!

LeBron's Mom

Frankie Walker and LeBron

LeBron's friendly coach was a
man named Frankie Walker.

Frankie and his wife Pam really liked LeBron and Gloria and
always wanted to help out where they could. Mr. Walker also
coached his son's 4th grade basketball team, the *Summit Lake
Hornets*, and signed LeBron up to play.

SUMMIT LAKE HORNETS

← LeBron and his mom (Gloria)

LeBron immediately fell in love with basketball.

He had a natural gift that others saw.

Mr. Walker helped teach him the fundamentals of the game and then LeBron would practice what he learned. He practiced and practiced. He practiced more than anyone else and when he practiced he would dream of some day playing in the NBA.

Gloria received some bad news. Her and LeBron were going to have to move *again*. Once Pam and Frankie Walker heard this they offered to help by letting LeBron live with them until Gloria was able to save up enough money and find a place for them both to live.

Gloria was very sad but knew that she could come and see LeBron whenever she wanted.

At the Walker's, LeBron had to wake up every morning at 6:30 to get ready for school.

He had to make his bed, keep his room clean and help out around the house. He also had to try hard in school and if he wanted to play basketball, he had to finish his homework first.

When he was done doing everything he had to do, LeBron was able to do what he wanted to do, and that was play basketball.

He would go outside and practice for hours, *everyday*.

LeBron didn't miss another day of school after that. He even found out that he *liked* going to school! His favorite classes were music, art and gym.

After school one day, LeBron's mom stopped by to see him. She had some very exciting news.

Thanks to the Walker's help, Gloria was able to save up enough money to get her and LeBron their own place!

They may not have had many things or a lot of money but LeBron and his mom had a lot of love. They loved each other very much.

LeBron told his mom all about what he had been learning in school and also about his dream of playing in the NBA.

Over the next few years, LeBron would play in hundreds of games and was gathering up many fans with his standout play on the court...

... but there was not a bigger fan of LeBron than his mom, Gloria!

LeBron played wide receiver

SOPHOMORE SEASON		
Catches	Yards	Touchdowns
42	752	11
All-state first-team wide receiver		
JUNIOR SEASON		
Catches	Yards	Touchdowns
57	1,160	16
All-state first-team wide receiver		

LeBron became a two-sport star playing both football and basketball in high school. He was fast, strong and could jump high, all things that made him an excellent receiver. He was one of the best receivers in the state of Ohio and many college teams offered him scholarships, including Notre Dame.

LeBron went to
St. Vincent-St. Mary's
High School in Akron, Ohio

But after his junior year, it was clear to anyone who ever saw LeBron play basketball that he would eventually play in the NBA, so he decided that he wouldn't play football his last year of high school and risk getting injured.

He had become a legend on the court and was twice named the best player in the *entire* country. People from all over would come to watch 'the kid from Akron' play basketball.

LeBron was such a gifted basketball player, that film makers detailed his young life in a movie and he was on the cover of *Sports Illustrated*, all while still in high school!

"KING JAMES"

It was in high school when LeBron was given the nickname "King James." He was the king of every court he stepped foot on.

Many began comparing him to basketball legend and his hero, Michael Jordan.

February 18, 2002
Sports Illustrated

That's LeBron in high school!

LeBron led the "Fighting Irish" to three Ohio state titles.

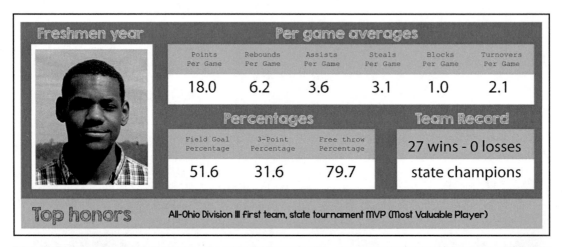

Freshmen year

Per game averages

Points Per Game	Rebounds Per Game	Assists Per Game	Steals Per Game	Blocks Per Game	Turnovers Per Game
18.0	6.2	3.6	3.1	1.0	2.1

Percentages

Team Record

Field Goal Percentage	3-Point Percentage	Free throw Percentage
51.6	31.6	79.7

27 wins - 0 losses

state champions

Top honors   All-Ohio Division III first team, state tournament MVP (Most Valuable Player)

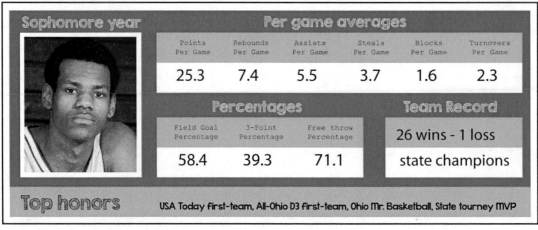

Sophomore year

Per game averages

Points Per Game	Rebounds Per Game	Assists Per Game	Steals Per Game	Blocks Per Game	Turnovers Per Game
25.3	7.4	5.5	3.7	1.6	2.3

Percentages

Team Record

Field Goal Percentage	3-Point Percentage	Free throw Percentage
58.4	39.3	71.1

26 wins - 1 loss

state champions

Top honors   USA Today first-team, All-Ohio D3 first-team, Ohio Mr. Basketball, State tourney MVP

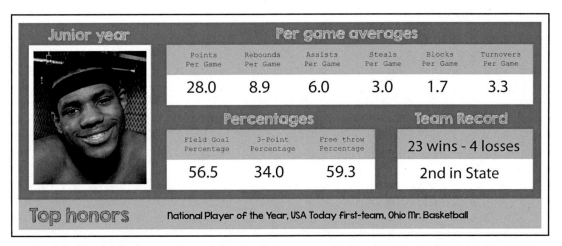

Junior year	Per game averages					
	Points Per Game	Rebounds Per Game	Assists Per Game	Steals Per Game	Blocks Per Game	Turnovers Per Game
	28.0	8.9	6.0	3.0	1.7	3.3

Percentages			Team Record
Field Goal Percentage	3-Point Percentage	Free throw Percentage	23 wins - 4 losses
56.5	34.0	59.3	2nd in State

Top honors — National Player of the Year, USA Today first-team, Ohio Mr. Basketball

Senior year	Per game averages					
	Points Per Game	Rebounds Per Game	Assists Per Game	Steals Per Game	Blocks Per Game	Turnovers Per Game
	30.4	9.7	4.9	2.9	1.9	2.8

Percentages			Team Record
Field Goal Percentage	3-Point Percentage	Free throw Percentage	25 wins - 1 loss
56.0	38.2	67.8	state champions

Top honors — National Player of the Year, USA Today first-team, Ohio Mr. Basketball, State MVP

After he graduated from high school, it was no surprise LeBron decided to go straight to the NBA. It was also no surprise that he was the number one pick in the *entire* NBA draft!

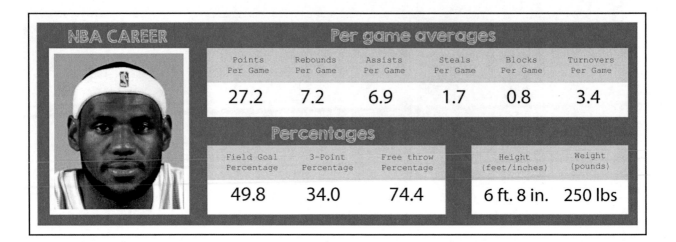

NBA CAREER	Per game averages					
	Points Per Game	Rebounds Per Game	Assists Per Game	Steals Per Game	Blocks Per Game	Turnovers Per Game
	27.2	7.2	6.9	1.7	0.8	3.4
Percentages						
	Field Goal Percentage	3-Point Percentage	Free throw Percentage		Height (feet/inches)	Weight (pounds)
	49.8	34.0	74.4		6 ft. 8 in.	250 lbs

The rest, as they say, is history. LeBron James has become one of the best, if not *the best* basketball player that the world has ever seen.

He is capable of dominating any game that he plays in, against any player, playing all positions on the basketball court from point guard to center.

LeBron James Career Awards

3 NBA Champion	3 NBA Finals MVP	2 Olympic Gold Medals	12 NBA All-Star
4 NBA MVP	12 All-NBA Team	6 All-NBA Defensive Team	2 All-Star Game MVP

He has won NBA titles, MVP's and award after award.

King James is already a legend, but there is one thing about LeBron that truly makes him a king, more so than anything he has ever done on the basketball court...

He cares about others. LeBron has never forgotten how hard it was for his mom and him when he was growing up. He is constantly helping those who have no money, no place to stay and little help.

The LeBron James Family Foundation was started by LeBron and his mom. It has helped thousands of struggling single parents and their children stay in school by providing places to stay, food to eat and schools to go to.

LeBron James' childhood dream came true and now he wants to help others to have their dreams come true too!

NEVER GIVE UP

Made in the USA
San Bernardino, CA
14 February 2017